Forevermore

Yeshua

In a world of dreams
And a world of illusions
There is only one reality.

Poetry Contents

Poetry Contents (cont.)

Epigramic Poetry Contents

Epigramic Poetry Contents (cont.)

Epigramic Poetry Contents (cont.)

Short Stories Contents

Poetry

Sadness

Will happiness find sadness...
Lay in a pool of dust

I could not find it
Find what I was
When I was going where I
Thought I wanted to be

What do I do when all that remains...
Sadness

Sadness inflicted
In a pool of dust where I sit
In an attempt to resurrect my own sincerity

Sincerity, though it may truly be sincere
Is so much so an attempt to find
An elevated purpose for happiness

It stays
And channels itself through
Unwilled self-priority

But priority never succumbs to
Happiness...
Nor happiness to my own inflicted sadness.

Bring Me Fainted Roses

Bring me fainted roses
They shall dance and laugh
And whisper to me, though
In their laughter you do not know it
They will love me so

Fainted roses bending
'Ere slightly, they
Will whisper to the wind
How in their dance they will cling to me
Call me dearest friend

Bring me fainted roses
Roses laugh and dance
In sun and bitter snow
In their dance they will whisper to me
How they love me so.

Always a Wrule

Always a wrule
Evergoing
Where I've been
Yet never knowing

Never knowing
Though ever see
What I've been
Shall ever be

Ever be
Yet never there
Though longing forever
Forever where

Always a wrule
Ever knowing
Yet never forever
Evergoing.

When Did You Go

When did you go
Where sulfur's so
So like fire
Fire and ice

You met your fate
A fate you met
When once you thought
You should forget

Forget the soul
With tainted lies
That whispered how
You thought divine

Divine though be
The God of love
Human kind
Seeks no reprove

When did you go
Though now you lie
So distant though
So forlorn time

Your fate you met
Did you know why
You cling to yet
Fire and ice.

Wish of Me

When you think, think of me
And I will wish

When you dream, dream of me
And I will wish

Though dare to say with woe
Tomorrow I shall not let go

When you wish, wish of me
And I will make it so.

Where is He

Mirages, mirror dances
And distant past images

Where is he
Whose hollow past forecloses

I was yet faltered
I beheld my own existence

When I was
Whose name was on self-mirrored images

I took what was left
I ravaged my own existence.

Hazy

No one knows but I found it
I found where you were
No one knows yet I found it

In the hazy reflection
Of your mind.

I Gaze at the Stars

You are when I wander
I wander near yet far

I wander and then falter
Relinquish my heart

I falter when I wander
Relinquish my heart

I gaze and then wander
I gaze at the stars.

This is All

I looked over the sea for changes
Hoping for distant changes
Hoping beyond hope

This is all.

What I last saw washed a memory
Of what could ever for ever be
Changes, distant changes

This is all.

And I know you could go forever
And ever never be
With a thought, it all over

This is all.

Love Judges Time

Love judges time
Not in hate or bitter words
Lest words disappear
Not in injustice
Though injustice often prevails

Love judges time
When time holds no justice to judge
God's sweet justice will prevail
In time, when time is set to glorify the justice of God.

Never We Believe

Never we believe:
In truth we say
We believe
But it never happens
The way that we think

Never we think:
The way that we believe
Is the way
That will lead us to the truth

What is truth:
The truth we seek
Is truth only
In name
Because what we believe
Is what we think we know.

Do I Remember

There are times
When I think of you
Only to remind me
Of my own self worth;

Isn't it sad
Only to become
Who I think
You may not be;

And I often wonder
At the hesitation
You provide
For what should be
Your greatest needs;

Do I remember
What satisfaction
You had
When you said
No one was to blame
For your own mistakes
But everyone.

Thoughts

Requiesence
Is a dream
Where I hope
And remiss
My laughter;

Tears
Are a thought of memoir
To renounce
Unwanted conclusions;

Daydreams
Are hopes received
During fantasy
Expectation;

My heart
Is a place
Where is accomplished
My deepest, and most sincere
Conclusions.

When

When everything I know
And everything that could be
Changes winter into summer

When all that I've seen before
Like a sparkle in the sand
Is released in time

Tears will flow
And wash away
To a river of hopes and dreams.

The Water

Open my mind
To placid lakes
Streams and rivers
Overflowing:
In its deepest generosity
The water sings
Like a lullaby
Sung over and over
By an ancient meadowlark
Still trying to find a tune
Most befitting to its kindness
It freely surrenders itself
To all the birds, trees,
And all life
That bathes, and drinks
And flourishes
From its compassion
When I observe
Its simplicity
I think that I
Would like to
Find serenity in its humbleness
And learn from
Its wisdom.

I Remember

I remember, still,
When you were
In a field of wildflowers
We walked
And talked
Of yesterday
And dreams of tomorrow
And you took my hand
And held me
And asked me not to forget
Today;

In your voice,
There was always
Laughter
And your smile
Gave reason
For the morning sun
To sparkle
Through your eyes:
And I would not forget.

The Wanderer

Your eyes are restless,
Sad realms of light
Exposing the bitter circumstances
That have invaded your life;

Your life is a search
Forever finding
What calls on you most
Through endless voyages;

Where will you go
Will you ever return
Rest from your wanderings
In an empty bed;

A dark shadow calls
And reveals itself
Through corners
And doorways of empty halls;

You've been alone many times
But do you really know who you are
Chase away the shadows
With the appearance of your own existence.

Dreams

There are times
When your sadness
Overfills the deepest
Part of you

And I wonder at how
You ever made it through
The darkest part of your world

At the edge
Of all eternity
You stand
Embracing
Your own expectations

Will you ever see
Morning and sunlight dreams
Beyond the midnight sky.

My Hope's Desire

Always praying
Forever cry
Always wanting
My hope's desire

Always searching
For the past
Left alone
Forever lost

Always seeing
What only I see
Never knowing
Another way

Never knowing
Or able to find
What I once only
Left behind

Always searching
Never knowing why
Always wanting
My hope's desire.

The Dance

The sun
With its rays of warmth
Sprinkles glitters of sunshine
Across the little valley;

I sit here in this little hideaway
By a tree that humbly gives me strength
And I witness
God's little creatures as they flutter
From branch to branch
And I wonder at how little
Their lives have changed all these years;

All that is alive
Sings and dances about me
And somehow I have become
A part of this little gathering
And I close my eyes,

There is an oncoming sound
That echoes and resonates
Through the skies
As the beat of distant drums
And drops of sea
Begin to fall upon my listless body,
It seems the thunderbeings
Have decided to join the dance,
They gather attention
From all that is and
That surrounds me
And if I listen to them very closely
I can hear them softly chanting a song
Of days past
When there were the echoes
Of voices and the laughter

Of a people who once were
A part of this beautiful dance;

After a brief moment of silence
The rain clouds have decided to part
Leaving behind only a portion of their gift
As a way of saying
Thank you for inviting me;

The sun, who is now bowing his head,
Brings his warmth gently
As if to say he must also be on his way
To other lands who long for his company;

And I
Who am now but half awake
And yet totally rested and filled with inner peace
Realize that I also must depart;

As I walk up the hill that has been
As a quiet observer in all that exists
And is,
I turn around
And feel the humbleness of God before me,
And I feel sad
To be leaving the dance
In these mystical canyons
Once Lakota Land.

My Reality

Awake,
With the bitter ages
For one moment in time
Then,
Bend beneath the willow
And touch the earth;

Come to me
In Your rest
I find
My life
And in Your hopes and dreams
I find
My reality.

Wishes

All my sorrows soon forgotten
Wind beneath my naked soul
Breath of life, it is inside me
Now I am forevermore

Behold my life
And draw tomorrow
Who am I my whispering friend
Who stands so tall, I see forever
Yet touch the earth, I live again

And you can know
My thoughts and feelings
Beyond a realm of unbound and free
Softly calling, the gentle wind will guide you
And grant you wishes in your dreams

When Winter's Past

Search for me
When winter finds you
Left me not
In morning light

Set free the tears
That grieved to find you
When faith was gone
And hope was night

Remember me
When 'neath the willow
Reborn in spring
With hope in sight

Yet was the chance
Left far behind you
When winter's past
Sought morning light

Ever Blooming Roses

Ever blooming roses
Sway back and forth with love,
Filled with Divine presence
Gifted from God above.

In every vibrant bloom
Is ever time and season,
Caught in wisp of present
Brought forth in time of reason.

Yet have I well then known
The scent each petal brings,
Tender with God's mercy
Renewed in holy spring?

Have I with love gained sight
Of every gift of season,
The roses brought to me
Sprung forth in time of reason?

Of each and ever rose
In rose spectrum I've seen,
Colors that shine His skill
Present themselves to me.

Ever changing season
The rose bush new caresses,
The fall return to spring
Set out from God of Presence.

Ever blooming roses
Sent from the God above,
Filled with omnipresence
Gifted with precious love.

Without Love's Caress

You pray
Seek guidance
Yet your prayer is unanswered

You ask
For time
Yet time gives you no questions
Why

Do your prayers
Remain hopeless

You hope
Without dreams
And without understanding
Why

Why there are no answers

Yet your heart is
Without love's caress

From one to another.

Tears
(To Remember)

Would tears be
To wash away our sins
Or tears be
To face the bitter cold
Of cruelness in society
That we to each
Our brother's hold;

If I find
But one answer
To wash the tears away
Would it be
The Lord's compassion
To everyone I pass
Along life's way;

And if I go
But kindly
And remember, with tears,
His tender kiss
That if I go out
Like Elijah
Will they remember this.

The Love of a Mother's Heart

The love of mother's heart
Is kindness when given away
Is strength when sheltering the sick and the broken-hearted
From the darkest of the long day;

The love of a mother's heart
Knows compassion in its gentleness
Remembering to give sympathy
In warmth and tenderness;

And always, with love,
And in each and every day
The love of a mother's heart
Will always remember to pray.

Bitterness, Compassion, Truth

Bitterness
Is a dark hallway
Filled with crevices
And corners
Leading to every room
Where light
Enveloped the past,

Compassion
Is a spark of fire
That rekindles a light,

Truth
Is a lamp
That burns in the middle
Of a room.
To extinguish the darkness.

You're Whispering

You're whispering
And the waves shy
From your presence

You're whispering
And when your presence is beheld
Broken dreams are mended
And hopes released
In the ocean's tide

And even though hope
Is your dream's heaven way
Yet still,
You fly
When the wind calls your name

You're whispering
and only the ocean hears
You pray.

The Gift

If all is a gift
And all given
Then who am I
And where will I find
My soul

I believe in
The Almighty
Who I will be
Is where I am going

And when I see
Beyond
My own existence
Is when
I know
I will have found
My home

And the gift
Given me.

Time

Time
Beckons me
Am I a memory,

Tear-stained glass
Recalls
My memory
And deepest thoughts,
All that was, is now
With no tomorrow,

I stand
Conclude
Remain in my self-worth
And give remembrance
Of who I was.

When It All Began

And so,
All is what it should have been,
At last;
When you walk away
Will you ever be so forgiving
That you will remember
Not to carry your pain with you;

And as you stair
At the windowpane
That has become your dearest friend,
What will you see;
Has it been so easy
For you to turn away
And forgive;

Tomorrow,
All will be lost;
And you will shoulder
The secrets
To yourself in your little hideaway;
Will your heart pretend
It has no meaning;
Will you remember what was,
And will it always be as
Refreshed and sought
In your memory
As when it all began?

Forever Lost

One dream
Is another's destiny
Only drawing conclusions
From a prepainted history

Wanting, yet not searching
An endless desire
Forgetting for moments
Regrets transpired

Never hoping, never dreaming
Never returning to the past
For answers to memoirs
Truly forever lost.

If I Could Journey

If I could journey
For beyond places and time,
What would I see;

Excavations
That resemble a past
And a history
Of what I may be;

Reason
Within my mind
Of never ending travels;
Hoping
And remembering
What I may become;

And who am I
In a world
Beyond my own understanding;

Tomorrow
What will I be
If I achieve
So much
As they have already been.

Epigramic Poetry

Hope

Hope
Is compassionate
Is built on dreams
Judges not
And gives love
As a gift to others.

Sentiment

Reestablish my sentiment,
Never remember to always forget,
Take the time
To believe in something,
Recognize
What is never ending.

Judge Not the Giver

Winded whispers and tainted thoughts
Miles and miles believe
Judge not the giver
'Till his words set free.

For You...

For you I stand
Elevated in your desires.

Set Free...

Set free
My tainted tainted
Thoughts in me
To find you
As you
Wanted them to be.

You Are...

You are
Who I am not
When I did not want you to be.

Love Vindicated...

Love vindicated
When I was too longing for its desire
Yet too unappreciated
To understand.

Stillness Lay...

Stillness lay, alone in silence
For today
Then crosses paths with shadowed 'morrow
To resolve dissolutions
That, never found, re quit yesterday.

Tomorrow...

Tomorrow I leave yesterday to forget today.

Conclusive Love...

Conclusive love
Was only
In your extinction.

When...

When
Is a place you go
To find where you were.

Remember Me...

Remember me
In distant gray
As shadowed awe
That passes 'way.

Though Distant Stars...

Though distant stars with day set free
Time still holds them next to me.

Places...

Places come places go
Places tend to be
For the one who for the moment
Places them where they be.

...Of Morning Dreams

Four rivers
Turn two stones
Break
Ocean tides
Relentlessly
In pursuit
Of morning dreams.

States of Existence

These two, states of existence:
One with the Lord, one without.

That which is within the soul sets precedence for the state of one's own
existence
And designates the path for one's own destiny.

Honesty Without Compassion

Honesty without compassion
Is another title for
Destructive criticism
Its only goal is
To belittle someone,
It is prejudice
In another form,
It does not seek truth
But makes assumptions
Based on non factual evidence.

Sunbeams

Brilliant sunbeams shine
Like radiant light
And dance in hallways
Whispering their existence
With gentle warmth
To all that cannot resist their presence.

The Spring

The spring
In its colored season
Remisses
The laughter
Of raindrops
To the earth
And beckons the call
Of every seedling
That has awakened
From winter sleep.

Snow

Snow glistens in the pale night
And calls reflections to my mind.

My Shadow

I stand
In the darkness
Of my own shadow

Never knowing
Or seeing
The reality
Of my
Own world.

Alone

Alone
And drifting, aimlessly
I separate
Myself
From the blinding sea
And under
The witness of the raging storm
I defy myself
To become who I am not.

Moments

Moments
Contemplating silentness
Without reason,
Unfounded wantonness,
Searching for
Desires
Beyond expectation,
Over-exceeding
Limitless emotion
Unbounded,
Never reaching
A destination.

In My Memoir

Time spent wandering
In precious moments

Tender teardrops
Relinquish memories

Reminisce yesterday
With changes of today
Each and every new beginning
A photo
In my memoir.

To Remember

I can only recollect
Once-forgotten dreams
When echoes of memories
From distant childhood years
Should choose to relinquish themselves
From a past
That would follow me
And carry me
To a future
I've still yet to remember.

Pale Yellow the Winter Sun

Pale yellow the winter sun
That hides the darkest night
Remembering glimpses of yesteryear
In its sparks of morning light.

When All Is Lost

Someone, somewhere
Knowing why
Clouds of darkness
Uncover my eyes

Dreams of daylight
Awaken in thought
Then come to me, unknowingly
When all is lost.

As...

As cold and damp the night
As fearless as the firelight
As bitter as the winter snow
That releases the sun's morning glow

As raging the storm in the midnight sea
All these things you were to me.

Teardrops...

Teardrops
Can only substantiate conclusions
Of our inner self

Reality personified
Is who we may
Decide to be
Regardless of
Who we are.

Hope is Helpless...

Hope is helpless
In its way
Never reaching for
Yet never fearing
What may have to be

Never relinquishing
Yet never knowing
What may have to come

Always reasoning with
Yet never truly understanding
What may have already been.

The Winter Storm

The winter storm
Crosses the sea
And gives way
To the tide
That flows anxiously
Before the morn
When the sun
Raises its head
And awakens
From its tender sleep.

And Yet

I could see
Your heart
Was in another place
And yet,
You still tried
To replace changes
With all your self-worth

Everything
Was all
You wanted it not to be
And yet,
You still
Believed.

Love...

Love is for reminiscing wishes,
And fantasies and dreams;

Reality is for giving conclusion
To what love may be.

Sandstorms

Sandstorm's
Rain clouds
Deter my eyes
Release
Rivers
Sacred lullabys.

The Victor

Sultry and wantonly
Casting my victory
Upon another's
Appointed descentry.

You Followed Me

You followed me
In deepest oceans
You followed me
Through river's streams
You followed me
When there was no one
Though, when I fell
You followed me.

A Stranger's Voice

A stranger's voice
Echoes
In a room of darkness
Forever trembles
My heart
And sadness remains.

In Winter Years

No goodbyes
Tomorrow's tears
Left behind
In winter years.

I Will Remember

I will remember
When winter's song
Will sing of the lost year

I will remember
When the rising sun
Will be a gift of morning light
Sadness is a journey
Of tomorrow's tears

I will remember.

Hopeful Worrying

Hopeful worrying
Never changes its mind
Never turns its direction
Nor knows its distinction
Before the setting sun.

Kindness

Kindness, in compassion's strength
Shows tenderness
That weakness cannot comprehend.

Is Your Answer

Is your answer
Written
In windows of sacred light
Touched
Before the dawn
Of empty souls
Dreaming
Of earthly flight.

Sometimes We Play

Sometimes we play
In river's streams
Finding happy memoirs
Of childhood dreams
In voyages
Of what we were to be.

Sacred Lies

Sometimes we kneel
Sometimes we cry
Sometimes with only
Sacred lies.

The Promise

Do Your tears stain
The cloudlet sky
If only to look upon
The rainbow
And wonder why

When remembering
The Promise
That You gave
Do You watch Your children
At play
In a compassionless way.

Alive

So little is left behind
In walls of darkness
And a concave past is left behind me

If I seek
To understand
All
By the worries that others keep
Then I have missed
What it is
To truly be
Alive.

Icicles

I hope to see you
In the cold rain
And I'm frozen
To see again

In bitter dark
Like icicles
I'm hanging
In dreams
And crying your name

And I'm frozen
To see again
And calling your name.

Search

The softest touch
Of gypsy moon
In winter's pale light
Search for warmth
Of Summer Sun
On a horse God painted white.

Yesterday's Reminding

Love, yesterday
Was stolen by today;
Tomorrow is for
Forever finding

In its path
The dream of today
In yesterday's reminding.

His Tenderness

In all that we exalt
Will we find
There is but ground
To worship on

And to look upon the sky
In all its glory
Will we see His tenderness.

Sojourn

Sojourn in the land of my freedom
Giving birth to causes of sovereignty,

Educating the blind, in guidance
Massiveness abounding,

Remembering always to reimburse justice
With endless compassion,

Never overpowering resistance
With uneducated reasoning.

Like the Rain

Love, like the rain,
Sprinkles and showers its affection
On all that has gained its admiration.

Puns and Epigrams

Compassion is wisdom that blinds those without conscience.

Passing judgment on another's soul is a fatal flaw of mankind.

Submission is godliness in its purest form.

Seeking justice without compassion is condemnation.

The act of compassion is empathy placed in motion.

Empathy should not be a mystery.

Love is gifted as it is also given. Judgment is the token of bitter wrath.

Hope is a reception of God's Grace.

Sulfur and ice, requiems of mind to bind time.

Ambiguous is night that clings to day.

Love but do not give way to love to a heart tainted with hate.

Disburse love with compassion not to reimburse where there is none.

Fill godliness not with superiority.

Exist in virtue where virtue does not exist.

Freely evolved love may evolve to become hate when hate may cast its shadow in love.

Recognize emptiness not as thoughtlessness while concluding its selflessness.

Dwell in love where love may abound but can not be found.

When love is blind, in your search for the truth you see the least when you love the most.

Time is spending thoughts to reconcile with my own destiny.

Bitterness begins with tainted love.

Dreams are places we go when we choose not to belong where we are.

I only remember in the deepest of sincerity and in the pain of my own reality what I chose not to forget.

Hope is a gift received by those with expectations far greater than believed predestination.

Evolve with love that love may evolve with time.

Time strays and may reimburse itself while drawing conclusions from its contents.

Inquisitions were made for borrowing time from illusions.

God is who He chooses to be be though He draws no line from simplicity.

There is no logic hesitation in preconceived fabrication.

Wrong regrets are only foresight for seeking future right.

Tomorrow becomes today when self-will imposes no restrictions.

Inflictions ravage circumstances left to blind revel.

Knowing is wanting in reverse while believing is seeing forward.

What is is not when what has been is gone.

Time is a gift scattered across illusions.

Finale

Seek not for what you want
But rather for what God would wish for you,
For it is in His reality
That eternal dreams come true.

Out of all that is laughter
With song and with dance,
In childhood we remember
Our own innocence.

Hoping you will find
Who I once was
Still remaining
Yet set free
I give you all
Yet gifted you.

Butterflies and dreams

Hope is the Daylight
That awakens my past thoughts,
Hoping in Sun's sweet kindness
To hope all that is not lost;

If I should find, in sweetness
My hoped for dearest Friend
Would Hope be here to guide me
With hope...The End

Short Stories

Love is something that many people believe they can define or have felt for others such as, for example, a mate, family member, or perhaps a friend. However, unlike the love that is often equated with man's ideology of love, God's love is forever forlorn as He looks over man's ideology of love. Scripture testifies to this love, but sadly, because mankind can often be lost in a culture that does not always comprehend the depth of God's love while many even go so far as to doubt His existence, they leave off the vary nature of His love. The gospel account of Luke tells of Jesus' teaching on how to love in a story that is commonly known as the Good Samaritan. By examining Luke's gospel story of the Good Samaritan and comparing it with other Scripture verses that speak of God's love, we can show that God is love, that love is portrayed in His actions, and that He expects humanity to emulate His love.

In Luke's story of the Good Samaritan, Jesus is approached by a lawyer who tries to "tempt" Jesus (Luke 10:25). It is likely this temptation was to test Jesus' ability to give righteous judgment based on the law. As Dr. Wilson, writer of the *JesusWalk Bible Study Series*, emphasizes, "The skilled teacher of the law is testing this unofficial, Gallilean lay teacher to see how well he will answer difficult theological questions." His question presented to Jesus is simple enough: "Master, what shall I do to inherit eternal life?" (Luke 10:25). It is Jesus' response to this question that leads to His telling of a beautiful story that defines how to initiate God's love to others. Jesus asks this lawyer what is defined in the Law pertaining to this question, and the lawyer responds to His question by quoting the Ten Commandments (Luke 10:26:37). Jesus confirms the lawyer's answer as accurate: "Thou hast answered right: this do, and thou shalt live" (Luke 10:28). This lawyer, however, was looking for more than a simple answer as a response from Jesus. Wanting to justify himself, he asks Jesus, "And who is my neighbour?" (Luke 10:29).

The lawyer need not ask any more questions because it is in Jesus' response to this question that the lawyer learns how God loves and expects others to love in one of the most beautiful stories told in the Bible (Luke 10:30). In Jesus' story, a man is traveling from Jerusalem to Jericho. On his journey, he is attacked by thieves, robbed, beaten, and left for dead. Both a priest and a Levite traveling on this same road see the injured man and pass by without helping him (Luke 10:31-32). After this, a Samaritan passing by sees the man and has compassion on him (Luke 10:33). He cares for his wounds then takes him to an inn where he gives this man further assistance (Luke 10:34). He then pays the owner of the inn to keep him there and give him further needed assistance until he could return (Luke 10:35). Jesus ends the story by asking the lawyer a question: "Which now of these three, thinkest thou, was neighbour unto him that fell among the thieves?" (Luke 10:36). The lawyer, recognizing there could only be one answer, replied, "He that shewed mercy on him" (Luke 10:37). It is then that Jesus, in one short sentence, tells the meaning of the story and how it is love is shown: "Go, and do thou likewise" (Luke 10:37). God's message of how to love one another is simple: humanity is to give compassion through their works toward others. It is not enough to say one has compassion for their neighbor. It is when someone shows that love by emulating the story of the Good Samaritan that they show their love for another to be genuine. A person does not need to go so far as to save another person's life to show this overpowering love unless it is necessitated. It is in one's daily life in how they put other people's needs before their own and consider another person's feelings to be more important than theirs that one has the ability to show God's love. It is, as Wilson notes, "a heart of mercy that is moved by compassion."

God's love is a selfless act which is best explained in John 3:16: "For God so loved the world, that he gave his only begotten Son, that whosoever believeth in him should not perish, but have everlasting life." God loves humanity so much that He was willing to give His Son's life in order to save the souls of humanity. With this gift of God's love, He asks that humanity return His love by enacting this self-same love to others. It can be something of less gravity such as giving a coat in need or running an errand, or it can be as serious as giving one's life to save another. The apostles and many other Christians have suffered martyrdom for this same reason. Though their charity (love put forth in action) can not give mankind salvation as did the Savior's gift, it shows their willingness to give their own lives if need be for the sake of others so that God can use them to further spread and teach His mission of love.

Dr. McFarland, professor in theology, explains another

philosophy on the story of the Good Samaritan. The Samaritan has been historically viewed within the Church as a representation of Jesus while the injured man represents all of humanity:

> In working out the implications of this latter point, it is worth recalling that throughout most of the church's history, the parable of the good Samaritan has been interpreted christologically. According to this reading, the man who falls among thieves represents humankind, seemingly dead from its sins; the Samaritan is Jesus, who brings us back to life as the persons we were created to be (McFarland 62).

Considering that at the end of the Story, Jesus tells the lawyer to "Go and do thou likewise," this understanding of the Good Samaritan shows that Jesus requires humanity to act in the same regards to each other as Jesus did for humanity

How God's love infiltrates the human heart was wonderfully presented by the apostle Paul in his first letter to the church at Corinth. Paul says he could have all kinds of gifts, such as speaking as an angel, the ability to prophecy, have "all knowledge" and "understand all mysteries" (1 Cor. 13:1-2), do works such as feeding others, and even give one's life as a martyr, but if any of these gifts or works are not accomplished out of genuine love for others, they are worthless: "I am nothing" (1 Cor. 13:3). God is calling humanity to not only enact the story of the Good Samaritan toward others but to genuinely feel that love for others within their own hearts. Paul goes on to say that love is a willingness to suffer for others, is selfless seeking being neither proud nor boastful, finds happiness in God's truth rather than sin (1 Cor. 13:4-6), and "'beareth,' 'believeth,' 'hopeth,' and 'endureth' all things" (1 Cor. 13:7). Though prophecies and other gifts may fail, love does not (1 Cor. 13:8). Paul's finality in urging the importance of charity (sincere love displayed in its actions) is that of the three, faith, hope, and charity, "The greatest of these is charity" (1 Cor. 13:13). Anything other than genuine love is nothing more than a clang of a "cymbal" (1 Cor. 13:1).

It is noticed in the Good Samaritan that Jesus equated showing love with keeping the Commandments (Luke 10:26-27). Further evidence of this is found in chapter 22 of Matthew and Mark chapter 12. In Matthew 22, a lawyer tries to tempt Jesus with this question:

"Master, which is the great commandment in the law?" (Matt. 22:35-36). Jesus' response is that the first and greatest commandment is to "love the Lord thy God with all thy heart, and with all thy soul, and with all thy mind" (Matt. 22:37) while the second after it is to "love thy neighbour as thyself" (Matt. 22:39). Everything written in "the law and the prophets" is defined and centered on these two commandments (Matt. 22:40). In Mark 12, Jesus is approached by a scribe who asks him, "Which is the first commandment of all?" (Mark 12:28). Jesus' reply is similar to that found in Matthew 22, except in this gospel he also quotes the Shema ("The Lord our God is one Lord"). This is significant because it shows Jesus is not giving a new law in how to love but is quoting the Hebrew Scripture (the Old Testament) to define God's love as it was intended to be between man and God since the beginning of creation.

Quoting chapter 6 verses 4-9, one can notice the similarity to that which Jesus told in Mark 12 verses 29 and 30: "Hear, O Israel: The LORD our God is one LORD: And thou shalt love the LORD thy God with all thine heart, and with all thy soul, and with all thy might." Mark agrees with Matthew in how Jesus said one is to love their neighbor "as thyself" (Mark 12:31). By comparing this verse to Old Testament Scripture, one can find that Jesus was again quoting Scripture: "Thou shalt not avenge, nor bear any grudge against the children of thy people, but *thou shalt love thy neighbour as thyself:* I am the LORD" (LEV. 19:18). Jesus' point in quoting Scripture that says to "love the Lord thy God with all thy heart" and to "love thy neighbor as thyself" is that love is shown by keeping the Commandments of God. To truly love and show that love to others, one keeps the Commandments of God by enacting the story of the Good Samaritan.

Because the actions of love are defined in the original Jewish Scripture, it was common during Jesus' time for the Jewish people to believe their "neighbor" whom they were to love "as thyself" meant their fellow Jewish people. But notice in the story of the Good Samaritan, the person who helped the injured man was not a fellow Jewish person such as the priest or Levite. Rather, it was a Samaritan. According to Dr. Jones, theologian, pastor, and New Testament scholar, "The Samaritans enjoyed the lowest rung on the social ladder following after despised trades, Jewish slaves, Israelites with a slight blemish, Israelites with a grave blemish, and Gentile slaves" (232).

Leitch, editor of *The Christian Bible Reference Site,* notes this about

the story of the Good Samaritan: "The lawyer was forced to admit that

it was the Samaritan who treated the injured man as a neighbor, not his

fellow Jews who did nothing to help." Jesus was making an important

point here: if one is to actually keep God's laws by "loving thy

neighbour as thyself," one needs to understand that "thy neighbour" is

not just the person who lives next door or those who belong to one's

own nationality. All of humanity belongs in this category of

"neighbour" which means one is to love all others and not judge them

by one's own standards. Leitch explains it this way:

> If a Samaritan could be a neighbor to a Jew, and Jesus
>
> told us to 'go and do the same,' then *all* of God's people
>
> must be our neighbors and we must love them just as
>
> the Samaritan man did! Yet, Christians, Muslims, Jews,
>
> Catholics, Protestants, Hindus, Buddhists, African
>
> Americans, Native Americans, Hispanics, Asians, the
>
> poor, the
>
> homeless, the unattractive, gays, lesbians, the
>
> handicapped, the mentally ill, and countless other

groups are still sometimes the victims of ridicule, hatred and discrimination. Jesus must be looking down with sadness that, after 2000 years, we have still not learned to love our neighbors!

Indeed it is a sad picture to think of Jesus, in all that He did for humanity, to be looking down at so many who claim to know his word but somehow do not seem to remember it in their daily engagements with others.

Jones takes this parable a step further by explaining that it shows significance in loving one's enemies because of the Jewish opinion of the Samaritans: "The scribe surely collided with his pride when he recognized the Samaritan as the hero and as one who could practice the Law of Moses, but he was extended far more to see that neighboring could mean loving your enemy" (235). This ideology coincides with Jesus' teaching in Matthew chapter 5 verses 43-44 regarding loving one's enemies.

It is in keeping obedience to this story that many can seem to get lost in modern times. Jesus' Samaritan story was not just for the Jewish people or those who lived in the first century. It was a story for all people in all generations to learn, understand, and to keep. Modern technology should make it that much easier for humanity to keep God's Commandments as outlined in the Good Samaritan. But is it instead used in ways to make the world that much more of a selfish place in which to live? Those who read Jesus' story need ask the same question Wilson asks:

> I must ask myself, what we -- as disciples of Jesus -- are supposed to learn from this story. And for me the answer is to examine my own heart. What motivates me? How much have selfishness and a dogged adherence to my own agenda leached away the mercy that Jesus holds dear and wants to flourish in my heart through his Holy Spirit? I may be efficient, but am I merciful. When "push comes to shove" do I put myself first, or do I put the needs of others first?

To properly address this question the answer is found by allowing God to motivate the human heart to respond to His love through charity (1 Cor. 13:13).

In summary, love is not something one seeks to gain for

themselves nor is it something to be taken from another. Love is not exposed through selfishly receiving but is imposed through sacrificial giving. When one learns how to love another with the love God requires, one seeks to prioritize the needs and concerns of another before one's own needs and concerns, whether it be to a family member, spouse, neighbor, close or casual friend, or someone unknown near or far. When a person loves with the love God calls them to honor, there is no room in the heart for hate; only love.

Works Cited

Jones, P. R. (1979). The love command in parable: Luke 10:25-37.

Perspectives In Religious Studies, 6(3), 224-242.

King James Version. BibleGateway. Retrieved from

http://www.biblegateway.com

McFarland, I. A. (2001). Who is my neighbor?: The good Samaritan as

a source for theological anthropology. Modern Theology, 17(1),

57-66.

Leitch, C.. The Good Samaritan. H. Leitch (Ed.). Retrieved from

http://www.christianbiblereference.org/story_GoodSamaritan.

htm

Wilson, R. F. #46. The Parable of the Good Samaritan (Luke 10:25-

37). Retrieved from http://www.jesuswalk.com/lessons/10_25-

37.htm

It was a long, cold day, but then aren't they all these days? Outside, the spring descended, its presence radiating as it attempted to reflect birth and life. But inside, in my heart, the cold set in, as chills that ran down my body, outward, and into the next generation. I began to question it all, where it all went wrong, past generations stealing everything that was called nation while leaving nothing behind but doubt. And what was this nation? What was it once called? Oh, yes, a nation of God. People began doubting everything, including God, and because of it a new religion crept in. Not unlike it's old counterpart, it marches in the name of war. But unlike its prepossessed ways, in its faith lurks a threat to everything that was called God. Its name is anti-love and anti-peace and in its ministry is a cruel dictatorship created to rob souls of their freedom. Al Qaeda, or is it ISIS, has become a mercenary of its victims.

My younger brother took a trip to the store, a trip much like any other. "Psst," he whispers. "Need anything? A can of soup will heal just as good as a vitamin." He jokes at my concern for this nation and for the world. Undoubtedly, he did not understand the pun in his words. Was it a vitamin for the soul he needed? Regardless, to him it went unrealized; nothing had changed. Freedom was secure and on our back doorstep. I wanted him to realize that freedom becomes tainted and loses its glow when its religion is flipped to the other side of tomorrow. Will he recognize he could lose it all, all that he has in the name of freedom, to this new cause?

Each soul must recognize their own fate. In recognition, each soul plays its part in a battle of good against evil. But evil can bounce in the brain like thoughts pulled by gravity from one side to the other. It is dissolved only by godly forces which consume the evil and bring the soul to a humble mental paradise. Without godliness, the evil forces remain as the force that dictates movement to the brain. The soul summons God, but there is no answer. Evil forces make their appeal to a higher evil and the soul becomes empowered by greater forces of evil (Matt. 12:43-45, KJV).

While evil controls its victims, godliness circumvents evil through compassion and brings the soul to repentance. Through repentance, godliness delivers the soul to God's grace where goodness flourishes and can abound with mercy. Mercy guides the soul and releases itself to the souls of humanity in the form of compassion which dictates the soul and restrains it from the forces of evil. Therefore, to keep humanity restrained from evil, godliness is needed; only then can goodness show its mercy. God removed, evil conquers the souls of humanity and adheres itself in a new religion.

A new religion has soaked the soils of humanity, making its way to the counterparts of the earth, and has become accepted by generations who held in disdain everything that was God. Eyes closed, it appears only to those sovereign while clouds continue to gather in streets. In the streets lurks a man who scorns his neighbor for simply being there. He is in a hurry and the horns honk, unkind words fly through his voice and dissolve themselves in a high pitched shrill that is as a sword crucifying the ears of its victims. Like so many, he has taken for granted his freedom.

Freedom is blessed. In its soil flows compassion to others who have found favor in its system. The owner and the worker together bring prosperity to their neighbor. So blessed, yet it goes unrecognized by many finding favor in false regime. If tomorrow causes their favor to collapse sovereignty, the world as we know it will give way to a parallel universe under which ISIS holds its grasp.

Questions left unanswered, I am left wondering. What will happen to the universe? Will this new cause bring chaos and with it forces of destruction? Will the earth dissolve from its forces? Should sovereignty fail, will this be the end of all that is truly God? Or will an evil parallel universe flip the course of evil and destroy it forever? Maybe the end will be just the beginning. Maybe a new cause brought about in the name of a godless religion will open the world's doors to God. The stars glimpse a dreary day that with its bitter cold will bring the warmth of spring.

Seeking Mary-Jane

When I was young and in my teens, I'd met up with a near-by neighbor who'd smoked. Now smokin' may not seem like such an important thing an' all, 'cept this neighbor didn't smoke those fancy chimneys they call cigarettes. Her favorite smoke was somethin' the law called marijuana. She liked to call it "Mary-Jane." She called it her best friend and said this friend was so helpful to her that her friend was somethin' like medicine. My neighbor was a near hefty and quite jolly sort an' I didn't feel no need to argue with her over such matters. Besides she had her share of difficult days jus' goin' through them she seemed like she was in such pain. 'Cept when her good friend Mary-Jane visited her, then she was all perked up an' smiles an' stuff.

My parents used ta' warned me 'bout this "Mary-Jane" and the dangers that could be ill gotten from things like drinkin' and doin' drugs. And they warned me 'bout sociatin' with the likes of anyone who would keep with such stuff fer a friend. They also warned me that if the law caught me with these friends, they would give me a Monopoly "Go to Jail" card. They told me that "Mary-Jane" was a bad friend to have and that I best avoid anyone who keeps company with the likes of her. My dad would say things like, "If you play in mud, don't be surprised if ya' get ya' some mud on ya'." My parents believed people who did illegals "played in mud," and they were worried that I might someday take up usin' some a this "mud" and it would dirty up my life. Maybe they were right. With the law, once you have a record of doin' somethin' law-breakin', that record stays with ya'. Bosses who find ya' have a record are a lot less likely to hire ya'. Couldn't blame my parents for being concerned. I knew my parents were right, a drug record in a small town could ruin a person's life.

Once, when I was talkin' to my Mary-Jane friendly neighbor, she told me why she was such good friends with Mary-Jane. She told me she had this cancer, a tumor in her brain she said. She said the medicine could stop the pain, and it also stopped some seizures the tumor was causin', better than anything the doctor give her. Well, when she told me why Mary-Jane was a friend, it got me thinkin'. Was Mary-Jane such a bad friend to have? Maybe this "Mary-Jane" wasn't really all so muddy.

As I got older, I really started thinkin' 'bout "Mary-Jane" more. It wasn't that I wanted her for my own friend. My parents had given me a mud mentality that kept me from usin' illegals. But I was no longer so sur' that just 'cause her personality was the type I didn't want for a friend that this made her all muddy. Maybe for some people she could keep a good friendship, maybe even an important and helpful one. So, I decided to do some research on Mary Jane an' guess what I'd found? I'd found some good qualities in this Mary-Jane. But I'd also found out why some others they weren't so fond of her.

What I found was "Mary-Jane" was disliked 'cause she was what law called "a gateway drug." They said people that smoked this gateway were more likely to use other illegals that were harmful like this heroin' and cocaine stuff. Also, I learnt Mary-Jane wasn't liked 'cause law said she brought out violent tendencies in people who used it, making them more 'sceptible to criminal activity. But then for some reason they later change their story and say now Mary-Jane is a good tonic and it can calm the nerves. They say this tonic can relieve things like anxiety and depression like what's found in people with violent tendencies. What puzzled me 'bout this information is that Mary-Jane nerve tonic they say is kept illegal for promotin' what they call violent behavior, even though they now say otherwise, and yet they keep alcohol legal when it likes to bring out ill behavior in a person.

So, I began doin' some more research and found Mary-Jane in what they call "peer-review studies" 'cause she was proved to have benefits like for Crohn's disease, glaucoma, aids, somethin' called Tourette's syndrome, this Huffington's disease, pain, schizophrenia and other kinds a' mental disorders ("60 Peer Reviewed Studies"). The studies they say Mary-Jane's positive 'ffects far outweigh the negative so Mary-Jane should be at least used 'fer some medicine.

Well, as I kep' a readin', I found out more 'bout those who didn't want this Mary-Jane to be a friend to anyone. They say 'spite these good medicine qualities in Mary-Jane, she has some bad ones too. They say she brings out the paranoias in individuals. But they didn't 'xplain how that this paranoia isn't near bad as those chemical drugs on the market that cause ya' to get paralyzed or die er' somethin'. Seems to me, compared to those side-effects from chemicals, Mary-Jane isn't so awful bad. "Cept the chemicals cure a body so much that they don't be a livin' to feel their sufferin' any longer.

'Nother thing I found out in my learnin' is this Mary-Jane can be a good friend for many other uses too like fer' makin' soaps, nets, food, wearables, bricks, lubricant stuff, lightin' oils, gas fer' some vehicles, furniture goods, ropes of sorts, paper, an' other things like that ("Cannabis"). Usin' Mary-Jane means no more gas buyin' from those foreigners. And since Mary-Jane can be grown every year, her paper-makin' could save forests from bein' exterminated. And Mary-Jane can do like trees an' clean up toxics from the environment. Also, Mary-Jane has some edible hemp seeds that can make some tasty an' cheap porridge that can help stop world hunger problems.

When I got thinkin' 'bout how Mary-Jane could be yummy an' yet good fer' makin' so much stuff, I began wonderin' why she wasn't made lawful. If they think she might get others in a hissy fer' her smoke smell, they could set up these "No Smoking" zones in different places to fix it. They could also put Mary-Jane in a pill so she's not a bother to those who don't want ta' be a 'sociatin with her friendliness.

Of course, fer' the world of big business, there could be further side effects 'cause the oil companies aren't a wantin' their profits competed by Mary-Janes' fuel makin' capabilities. Also the pharmaceuticals wouldn't be a wantin' the likes of Mary-Jane takin' 'way from them their business profits.

What I got from my Mary-Jane learnin' is that Mary-Jane could be a useful and even a good friend to have. But I'm a hopin' fer' my own sake I won't be a needin' to call on her fer' a friend. "Cept maybe she could make me some fine furniture or somethin'.

Works Cited

"60 Peer Reviewed Studies on Medical Marijuana." *ProCon.org*.

Retrieved at http://medicalmarijuana.procon.org/view.resource.

php?resourceID=000884. Accessed 4 May 2017.

"Cannabis Is the Most Versatile, Efficacious Plant on Earth."

Cannabis Campaigners Guide. Retrieved at http://www.cc

guide.org/uses.php. Accessed 4 May 2017.

I, Paul, Speak at the Areopagus

The hillside where the Areopagus resides is a place located in the city of Athens "renown for sharing and debating various philosophical ideologies (Acts 17:21 [NIV]). It is here that I, Paul, have decided to present a speech to those worthy hearers. Though my former speeches have been heard by the Jewish and gentile trained in Scripture, at the Areopagus I will speak to the idol worshiper and philosopher.

My fellow believers have only recently escorted me to Athens. Forgoing excursions in several cities and various regions has caused riots on my behalf, and much pain and suffering through it, and my removal. I have just come from the city of Berea for the same reason. Currently, I await the arrival of my two dearest friends, Silas and Timothy. Do I dare say they are more dedicated to the Lord than I? They have been a great deal of help to me.

While waiting for the arrival of my friends, I have decided to take a stroll around the city of Athens. I have noticed the many forms of idols on display for worship and am "greatly distressed" at what I have seen (Acts 17:16). I begin to make daily visits to the marketplace in hopes that I will be able to share the gospel with those innocent to learn.

Upon arrival at the marketplace, I have introduced myself to those who call themselves philosophers. Like myself, they do not agree with the many forms of idol worship in the city. By name, they are Epicurean and Stoic philosophers (Acts 17:18). I begin to share my message with them, but they seem to be left with the impression I am speaking of some foreign god. I must seem to them as a babbler of some sort, someone who talks of hearsay but is not all that familiar with his religion. Still, they are interested in hearing more of what I have to say and they invite me to meet with them at the Areopagus (Acts 17:19), an opportunity for which I am delighted.

At the Areopagus, I begin speaking to the crowd that has gathered around me. Although I have found the idol worship of the city to be disturbing, I complement their desire to worship. "People of Athens! I see that in every way you are very religious" (Acts: 17:22).

As I continue my speech, and aware of those present such as the Stoics and the Epicureans, I decide to relate to those philosophers beliefs of which I have in common and perhaps those not so common.

Unlike the idol worshipers of the city, the philosophers do not believe in the "gods of ancient myths" (Fernando). They believe in an unseen God. And while the Epicureans believe this unseen God not involved in creation, the Stoics believe God created out of logic, as a a forethought determined by fate (Fernando), which would give structure to the universe "by which men ought to live" (Marshall). I will not stray from Scripture. I will present to them the God that exists as He is.

As I reason with them, I explain it is this unknown God, Creator and Giver of life to all that exists, of which I speak, "So you are ignorant of the very thing you worship—and this is what I am going to proclaim to you...The God who made the world and everything in it is the Lord of heaven and earth and does not live in temples built by human hands. Rather, he himself gives everyone life and breath and everything else" (Acts 17:23-25). Where I disagree with the philosophers, I choose "the writings of their own philosophers" (Fernando) to prove a their idocracy. If it is true that "in him we live and move and have our being" and "we are his offspring" (Acts 17:28), then God is not far removed from mankind; God "is not far from any one of us" (Acts 17: 26-27).

Thus far, I, Paul, have shown their own philosophy to prove idol worship false, "since we are God's offspring, we should not think that the divine being is like gold or silver or stone—an image made by human design and skill" (Acts 17: 29). I have hoped to gain their understanding.

The God who is involved in the affairs of man, I tell them, has understood their past frailty, "In the past God overlooked such ignorance, but now he commands all people everywhere to repent" (Acts 17:30). Man's own ignorance of God has excused their past, but His Son has come into the world to set things straight and offer redemption in place of ignorance. If they require proof that God exists, they need only to look to the resurrection.

I have finished debate with the philosophers. Do they still think of myself less learned than they? I warn them, God has "set a day when he will judge the world with justice by the man he has appointed" (Acts 17:31). Will they choose to listen?

Among those who have become followers are Dionysus, (an associate of the Areopagus), a woman named Damaris, and a score of others (Acts 17:34). My Athenian speech has not been without reward.

Works Cited

Fernando, Ajith. *The Acts NIV Application Commentary.* Grand Rapid: Zondervan, 1998.

Marshall, I. Howard. *Acts : Tyndale New Testament Commentaries Volume 5.* Downers Grove: InterVarsity Press, 2008.

My Precious Friend

Sometimes we see in shades of gray. I was like that for awhile, not sure what life expected of me nor I of it. But all that change in a moment, in the twinkling of an eye. I like to use that phrase because it speaks of the resurrection of souls. For me, there was no other way to explain it.

The resurrection was like other biblical information, the Bible itself a household declaration in the country home of my upbringing. Quaint and shabby, we did not own a whole lot of anything. The land was still in the ownership of my forefathers and hand-me-downs and used goods was a custom. But God was important, and it was important to my father that we understand that.

My father was a humble sort of fellow, a gent but not holding sway to customs. He was raised in a farming community and liked to talk about stories and teachings from biblical Scripture. In his words, he would leave behind worthy pieces of remembrance. He would say things like "You can't take it with you." about material goods. An old cliché? Maybe, but a Christian cliché none-the-less. My father would also say "The more wealth you get from the world, the more you want the wealth instead of God." I guess we had God's wealth and that made us wealthy in our land of poverty. But I didn't understand God's wealth at that time.

One day while I was rehashing in the blank areas of my mind where I searched for what I didn't have but thought I needed (which became a visiting habit), I remembered something I was told by my father about church. He'd say, "you can make good company there in church and visit fine about the Lord but a person didn't have to go to a church building to find God." And then he would say things like "If you want to talk to God, go out to the hills. You'll find him there." My father didn't have anything against attending a good church meeting but seemed to always find himself too busy with the outdoors work and trying to hold down a full time job and all. And since we didn't make a habit of going to church, I sometimes wondered if I could ever find God because of it.

Now, the more I felt a lingering deprivation for all those worldly goods I didn't have but thought I needed, the more I began thinking about asking God for them. (God was my alternative choice for acquiring goods as I knew I wasn't going to get them from family.)

I figured if God was really God then He could get them for me and so I began going to those hills to find Him. And that's what I did. I would go out to the hills and tell God everything I wanted that I did not have. I would ask for nice things and clothes and play stuff. I wasn't self-absorbed in my wishful wealth search. I asked if someday I could serve Him by helping others and I would tell Him how I'd like to write all kinds of good stuff for Him.

Pretty soon when that stuff didn't start to come my way, I got thinking maybe I was doing something wrong and maybe God would explain to me what that was if I picked up the book where He tells us stuff He wants us to know. I thought "If God is God, He would want to take good care of me and give me stuff and make me happy and He would want to tell me how He would do that." So, I picked up the Bible and started reading it.

When I first started reading God's words, I found it to be hard to understand. I kept trying to get past the thee's, thou's, and thou's just to try and make sense of the rest of it. (I had the King James Version). As I slowly crept through some areas of the New Testament book, like a turtle moseying it's way through rocky soil, I ran across a verse that said we need to be baptized. I got thinking maybe that's where my problem was. If I wanted to speak with the Lord and request His blessings, I needed to be baptized. But here was my dilemma. To get baptized, I needed to go to a church building. Since it seemed impossible for me to get to a church anytime soon (living miles apart from city living), I decided I best tell God my dilemma and how I want baptized and maybe He would understand my dilemma and baptize me best He can. So, I put down that good but hard-to-understand Book I was reading and told God "Well, Lord, my church is in the country. I talk to you in these hills and I want to keep on talking to you. But you say I need to be baptized and since I don't go to a regular church and have no way to get baptized in these hills, would you please baptize me?" You see, I didn't really realize what I was asking for. But God knew what I was asking for and he knew I needed His presence and that's why He lead me to read that baptism Scripture. He wanted me to ask Him to baptize me so I could be baptized His special way. Not the water immersion, though that is important when a soul finds God. God intended to baptize me in the Spirit.

Something happened that day and I was changed. From that

moment on, I was different, in the twinkling of an eye. It's a secret what happened to me when I talked to God and hardly a soul knows about it. For now, I want to keep it that way. Maybe some day I'll tell about it if for some reason God wants me to, but that would be for another story. I can say this much: I had a friend I talked to and that friend became my precious friend.

After my experience, things changed. I'd changed and what I knew and was beginning to learn changed with it. As I picked up the Bible and starting reading, there I was, speed-reading through it like it was my first language. I was understanding what the thee's, thou's, and thou's meant. Before my prayerful experience, I couldn't make much sense of it and now it was all beginning to take shape in my mind. It was like I had been walking through a hazy storm and found God's visible light on the other side. The fog had been lifted from my eyes.

I was 12 when I found God and Scripture became a special way my precious friend would visit me. I could feel His presence teaching me. Everything I was reading, I was learning what He was saying in His words as I was reading them. It was as if God would light up each page for me to read and show me what He meant it to say with each reading, The more I read, the more I could understand and the more I understood, the more I seen His light. God's truth was shining in that light. What I seen was His untainted sacrificial love. His light appeared to me in vivid colors of pastel.

Each word, every little detail in His Word, was a bite of spiritual knowledge, a tasty feast shared with Adam and Eve in the garden. There I was with the God of heavens as paradise took me down a new diminsion and gave me a dwelling. I didn't want to leave. Every day I looked forward to another imaginative walk through the garden. Everything I was learning, it was as if Jesus was leading me through the holy hills of paradise and sharing it all with me. I craved it. There was so much to learn. I couldn't get enough of God and He was the center of my universe.

Studies and homework, chores, that kind of stuff kept me busy most of the time. But whenever I got my chance, I would run to paradise. I lived for it and my existence outside of it was only mundane in comparison.

God remained my center-piece until I graduated and got work. It was a big move for me, going to the city after living my life in the country. Country life was all I'd known until then and it was a simple sort of life, peaceful and unrefined.

City life was like a drama, like taking a detour to the fast lane. Store runs were simple and quick and the housing experience saw a modern overlay of conveniences. But the more I became absorbed into the city, the further I became distanced from God. I did attend churches and found friends, and I recognized God's presence there in congregating with fellow believers. Yet, I felt an emptiness. Beyond the emptiness, I resolved to serve God, and in due process I reaped the rewards for my behavior. Vicious is the world when God is introduced to souls who resent His presence. Did I let my wounds take me down from His cross? No. But the enemy plays his cards well. My witnessed suffering of souls and lingering lonliness for His presence became inverted and in the process, I found myself becoming servant to ungodliness. In repentence, I searched for His presence and in the process, I felt as if I had lost my best friend. I wanted what the city life could not offer.

In the hills, with the sun rise and the peak of innocent days beckoning nostalgia, I found my way back to the country but so much had changed. My father's tractor accident ensured his safety was with the Lord now and much of the place had become antique. Still, the country itself was there and with it the hills. I remembered my father telling me "If you want to talk to God, go to the hills."

So, there I was again in those hills searching for my friend. I wanted to find Him again. I wanted to reverse time. I wanted what now seemed like ancient walks of paradise. So much had happened in my life since.

The move back to the country was uncomplicated. Still, questions remained. Were the paradise journeys lost to the past? Could I find God as I once found Him? Searching for Him felt as if I were searching for an oyster pearl in the oceans of heaven though a pearl of great price.

Through prayer and Scripture study, I sought to rekindle my connection and in the hills, I found my Savior smiling graciously and calling my heart to enter in to His presence. Once again, Scripture began to reveal itself, this time more vivid than when I was a spiritual child. My Savior had not forgotten me. He was there waiting for my return with hope that swept through His eyes and into my soul as a still voice calling through a cool breeze on a hot summer day. The last several years of my life have been given to God and lived through His presence.

I have to move again. This time I have no choice. Things have changed and I can no longer stay. Is it time for me to go? Did He intend to carry me through a rekindled friendship only to cast me back in to the shadows of the world? The answers lay asleep and await a future awakening. But I now know that no matter where I go, all the wealth and whatever this world has to offer could not part me from my precious friend. In a moment, in the twinkling of an eye, it's as if I'm there with him again.

www.ingramcontent.com/pod-product-compliance
Lightning Source LLC
Chambersburg PA
CBHW072208280526
45788CB00002B/928